PLANET UNDER PRESSURE
WATER

Louise and Richard Spilsbury

Heinemann Library
Chicago, Illinois

© 2007 Heinemann Library
a division of Reed Elsevier Inc.
Chicago, Illinois

Customer Service 888-454-2279

Visit our website at www.heinemannlibrary.com

Designed by Monkey Puzzle and Jane Hawkins
Printed in China by South China Printing Company

11 10 09 08 07
10 9 8 7 6 5 4 3 2 1

Library of Congress Cataloging-in-Publication Data
Spilsbury, Louise.
    Water / Louise and Richard Spilsbury.
       p. cm. -- (Planet under pressure)
    Includes bibliographical references and index.
    ISBN-13: 978-1-4034-8214-3 (library binding (hardcover))
    ISBN-10: 1-4034-8214-4 (library binding (hardcover))
    1. Water--Environmental aspects--Juvenile literature. 2. Water-supply--Juvenile   litera-
ture. 3. Water use--Juvenile literature. 4. Hydrologic cycle--Juvenile literature.   I. Spilsbury,
Richard. II. Title. III. Series.
    TD345.S68 2006
    333.91--dc22
                                2006016935

Acknowledgments
The author and publisher are grateful to the following for permission to reproduce copyright
material: Alamy pp. 7 (foodfolio), 30 (Dinodia); Corbis pp. 8, 22 (Amit Bhargava), 36 (Reuters);
Empics p. 27 (AP); FLPA pp. 34 (David Hosking), 38 (Frans Lanting), 41 (Terry Whittaker); Getty
Images pp. 6 (AFP), 10 (AFP), 13 (Time & Life), 14 (Ken Fisher/Stone), 16 (Andrew
Errington/Stone), 17 (PhotoDisc), 18 (David Driend/Image Bank), 24, 25, 28, 29 (AFP), 32, 33
(Aurora), 37 (Time & Life), 39 (AFP), 40; Interflush p. 31; MPM Images p. 35 (Digital Vision);
NHPA p. 12 (Martin Harvey); Panos Pictures p. 19 (Jean-Leo Dugast); Still Pictures p. 26 (Mark
Edwards); WaterAid pp. 20, 21. Maps and graphs by Martin Darlison at Encompass Graphics.
Cover photograph of boys collecting water reproduced with permission of Getty Images (AFP),
and of Iguazu Falls with permission of Still Pictures (Ron Giling).

Every effort has been made to contact copyright holders of any material reproduced
in this book. Any omissions will be rectified in subsequent printings if notice is given
to the publisher.

Contents

Any words appearing in the text in bold, **like this**, are explained in the Glossary.

Water Use Around the World

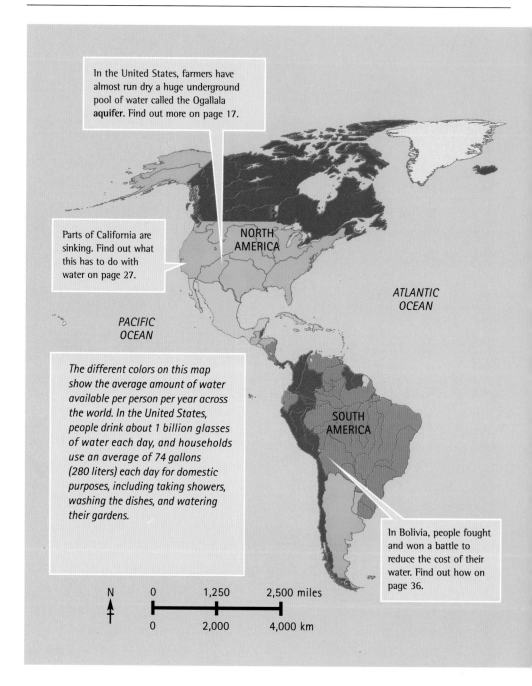

In the United States, farmers have almost run dry a huge underground pool of water called the Ogallala **aquifer**. Find out more on page 17.

Parts of California are sinking. Find out what this has to do with water on page 27.

NORTH AMERICA

ATLANTIC OCEAN

PACIFIC OCEAN

The different colors on this map show the average amount of water available per person per year across the world. In the United States, people drink about 1 billion glasses of water each day, and households use an average of 74 gallons (280 liters) each day for domestic purposes, including taking showers, washing the dishes, and watering their gardens.

SOUTH AMERICA

In Bolivia, people fought and won a battle to reduce the cost of their water. Find out how on page 36.

N

| 0 | 1,250 | 2,500 miles |

| 0 | 2,000 | 4,000 km |

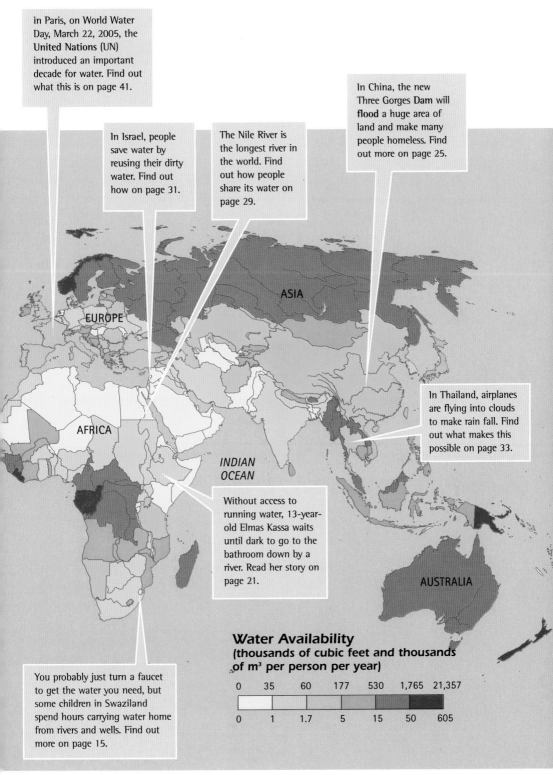

in Paris, on World Water Day, March 22, 2005, the United Nations (UN) introduced an important decade for water. Find out what this is on page 41.

In Israel, people save water by reusing their dirty water. Find out how on page 31.

The Nile River is the longest river in the world. Find out how people share its water on page 29.

In China, the new Three Gorges Dam will flood a huge area of land and make many people homeless. Find out more on page 25.

ASIA

EUROPE

In Thailand, airplanes are flying into clouds to make rain fall. Find out what makes this possible on page 33.

AFRICA

INDIAN OCEAN

Without access to running water, 13-year-old Elmas Kassa waits until dark to go to the bathroom down by a river. Read her story on page 21.

AUSTRALIA

You probably just turn a faucet to get the water you need, but some children in Swaziland spend hours carrying water home from rivers and wells. Find out more on page 15.

Water Availability
(thousands of cubic feet and thousands of m³ per person per year)

0	35	60	177	530	1,765	21,357
0	1	1.7	5	15	50	605

Source: UNEP World Resources Index

The World's Water

Earth is often called the "blue planet" because almost three-quarters of its surface is covered in water. Salty seawater makes up 97.5 percent of this and is virtually useless to us. Only 2.5 percent of water is freshwater that we can use, and two-thirds of this is trapped as ice, for example in **glaciers**, while almost all the rest is underground. Less than 0.8 percent of the planet's water is available to humans. That's the equivalent of just three teaspoons out of a half-gallon (2-liter) bottle.

A limited resource

Our supply of water is a finite, limited resource. The water on Earth today is part of the same hydrological or water cycle that has supplied our planet with water for two billion years. In the water cycle, the Sun's warmth causes water to **evaporate** from Earth's surfaces. When the **water vapor** rises into cold layers of the atmosphere, it **condenses** and turns back into droplets of water that form our clouds. Gradually, more water condenses on the droplet and it may collide with others, increasing in size until it falls to Earth as **precipitation** (rain, snow, or sleet). This eventually collects in rivers and lakes or runs to the ocean and the cycle starts again.

Ensuring that people across the world have the water they need in the future is one of the biggest challenges facing the world today.

A thirsty world

Water made life on our planet possible and it is vital to all human life. Today, however, 1.1 billion people do not have access to all the drinkable water they need. One billion makes up about one-sixth of the total world population—or, if you think of it in terms of a grade at school, one grade out of every six grades in the school. Serious water shortages affect communities in over 80 countries across the world.

Under pressure

Not only is there not enough water for everyone, but the demand for water across the world is increasing every year. It's not just a case of a growing population. Since 1950, the world's population has doubled, but demand for water is six times greater. We use more water because, in consumer societies, we buy more things, use more power, and eat more food, all things that require water. Over the next two decades, water use is estimated to increase by about 40 percent. To make matters worse, the amount of water actually available to us is being reduced by **pollution**.

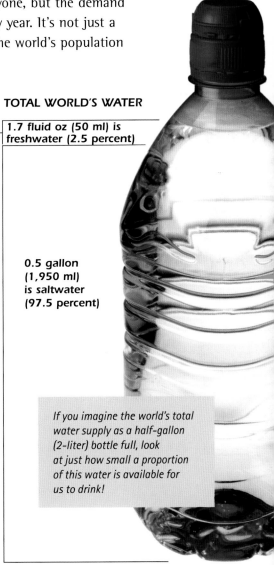

TOTAL WORLD'S WATER

1.7 fluid oz (50 ml) is freshwater (2.5 percent)

0.5 gallon (1,950 ml) is saltwater (97.5 percent)

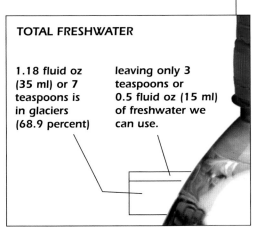

TOTAL FRESHWATER

1.18 fluid oz (35 ml) or 7 teaspoons is in glaciers (68.9 percent)	leaving only 3 teaspoons or 0.5 fluid oz (15 ml) of freshwater we can use.

If you imagine the world's total water supply as a half-gallon (2-liter) bottle full, look at just how small a proportion of this water is available for us to drink!

How much water do we need?

The human body can last weeks without food, but only days without water. Water makes up 50–70 percent of your body. It is found in fluids, such as blood and digestive juices, and within every cell—even in bones. Your body cannot store water, so you need to drink more each day to replace water lost from body processes such as breathing, sweating, and urination. Drinking six to eight glasses of water a day helps your body to function properly.

DRYING UP

If we don't drink enough water, the systems and organs within our bodies become less efficient, and eventually shut down completely. **Dehydration** occurs when you lose one percent or more of your body weight as a result of fluid loss. A small amount of dehydration makes you clumsy, tired, and moody, and makes it hard to concentrate. A loss of more than ten percent of body fluid weight is dangerous. People stop urinating, their kidneys fail, and they die.

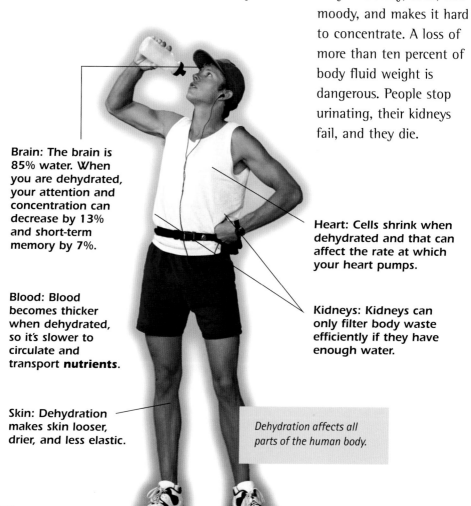

Brain: The brain is 85% water. When you are dehydrated, your attention and concentration can decrease by 13% and short-term memory by 7%.

Blood: Blood becomes thicker when dehydrated, so it's slower to circulate and transport **nutrients**.

Skin: Dehydration makes skin looser, drier, and less elastic.

Heart: Cells shrink when dehydrated and that can affect the rate at which your heart pumps.

Kidneys: Kidneys can only filter body waste efficiently if they have enough water.

Dehydration affects all parts of the human body.

WATER USE

To work out the amount of water a person uses, you need to count more than just the water they drink. All the water we use when we take a shower, wash the dishes, or flush the toilet counts, too. But there is even more to it than that. Farms and factories use massive amounts of water to produce the food we eat and the goods we use. When you take household, agricultural, and industrial water use into account, the average amount used by someone living in the United States is 500,000 gallons (1.7 million liters) a year. That means a family of four uses enough water each year to fill more than two and a half Olympic-sized swimming pools!

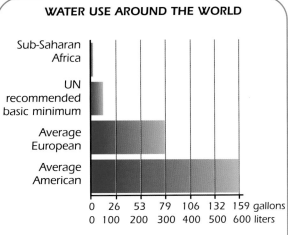

WATER USE AROUND THE WORLD

Sub-Saharan Africa

UN recommended basic minimum

Average European

Average American

| 0 | 26 | 53 | 79 | 106 | 132 | 159 gallons |
| 0 | 100 | 200 | 300 | 400 | 500 | 600 liters |

This chart shows the average water use around the world in gallons (liters) per person per day. In Europe, water use varies between 66–92 gallons (250–350 liters) per day.

Source: World Water Council

What you can do

- Ration your water use! Never put water down the drain that could be used to water plants or the garden, or for cleaning the car.
- Encourage your family to plant native or **drought**-tolerant plants that don't need frequent watering and should survive dry spells.

Where do we get our water?

The water we use comes from surface freshwater sources—such as streams, rivers, lakes, ponds, and **reservoirs**—and underground or **groundwater** sources. Globally, there is enough water for everyone, but it is unevenly distributed. Some countries are in arid (dry) areas that get very little rainfall. Two-thirds of the world's population live in areas that get only one-quarter of the world's annual rainfall.

RIVERS, LAKES, AND RESERVOIRS

Many rivers and streams begin high up in mountains and hills. Rain and melting snow runs off slopes and gathers in streams and rivers. A **river basin** is the entire area of land from which water or **run-off** drains into a river and its tributaries. Lakes and ponds form when rivers flow into natural dips in the land. Reservoirs are artificial lakes that people build to collect and store water from rivers or rainfall.

To extract groundwater from **aquifers**, for example through wells, people have to drill down to the level of the **water table**.

GOING UNDERGROUND

Groundwater is the main source of drinking water for one-third of the world's population, and it is the only source of water for rural people in many parts of the world. It forms when rain and snowmelt seep below the ground and gather in gaps in the rock, forming underground pools or streams in **porous** rocks (rocks that contain many small holes). Rock containing groundwater that supplies wells and springs is called an aquifer. The water table is the level below which soil and rock are saturated with water, and it is the uppermost level of a source of groundwater.

Water shortage

Today, about one-third of the world's population lives in countries where water is in short supply, but this could increase to two-thirds within 25 years as populations grow and demand for water increases. In many countries in Africa, the problem is too little rain all year round. However, in many Asian countries, such as India, rain falls heavily in a short season called the **monsoon**. During a monsoon so much water falls in such a short time that it doesn't have time to soak slowly into the ground. Instead, water runs off the land quickly into rivers and then the ocean, so little can be stored or used properly.

WATER SHORTAGE AROUND THE WORLD

This map shows those regions of the world where water is in short supply. Note that the blue lines mark the world's major rivers.

Source: UNEP World Resources Index

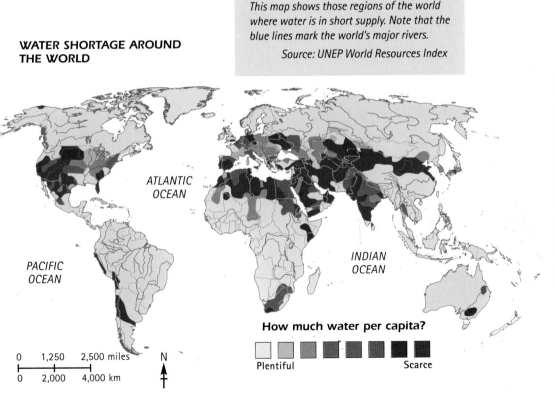

ATLANTIC OCEAN

PACIFIC OCEAN

INDIAN OCEAN

How much water per capita?

Plentiful   Scarce

0   1,250   2,500 miles   N

0   2,000   4,000 km

In the past, building a settlement by a river in a dry, hot country such as Morocco, in North Africa, was the only way to ensure that people had a regular water supply.

How do we get water?

If you look at a map—of the United States, for example—you'll notice that many settlements have been built alongside or around rivers. Early humans had to live near rivers and lakes to get water to drink, bathe in, to water crops, and for travel. Today, in the more-developed countries of the world, water may travel hundreds of miles through pipes and be carefully cleaned before it reaches people's homes.

How does water get to our homes?

In developed countries, when water is taken from rivers, lakes, or reservoirs, its first stop is a water treatment center. Here, the water is cleaned and purified. It is then either pumped, or it travels naturally down slopes, through supply pipes to a covered storage reservoir. When required, the water travels through smaller mains pipes to reach networks of pipes in cities, towns, and villages. In flat countries, there may be a series of pumping stations to help move the water along its route.

How is water cleaned?

At a water treatment center, water is cleaned and purified in several stages. First, it is screened to remove large bits of debris. Then, it is stored to allow medium-sized bits to settle so they can be removed. Next, the water is filtered through a layer or "bed" of material, such as gravel, to remove particles of dirt. It is treated with ozone and chlorine to remove **bacteria**, and passed through carbon to remove impurities, such as **pesticides** (chemicals used on farms), which could affect the taste and smell of the water. Finally, it is stored and ready to use.

This is a filter bed in a giant water treatment plant in the United States.

Water Today

The amount of water used by people in their homes, to produce the food they eat and the things they buy, varies greatly around the world. Household demand, particularly in cities, is rising rapidly as consumers use more water-guzzling household and garden appliances. There is also a lot of waste. Dripping faucets and leaking pipes in homes waste more water than is used for drinking and cooking!

AROUND THE HOUSE

The amount of water we use at home accounts for only about 10 percent of total global water use, but domestic water is vital for **sanitation** and health. In a more-developed country, such as the United States or France, the average person uses 26–53 gallons (100–200 liters) of domestic water a day. Of this, around 5 percent is used for cleaning, 10 percent for drinking and cooking, 20 percent for laundry, 30 percent for flushing the toilet, and 35 percent for bathing. In a less-developed country, such as Ethiopia, a person might have as little as 0.26 gallon (1 liter) of water a day.

Globally, on average, rich people pay a far lower percentage of their wage on their water than poor people.

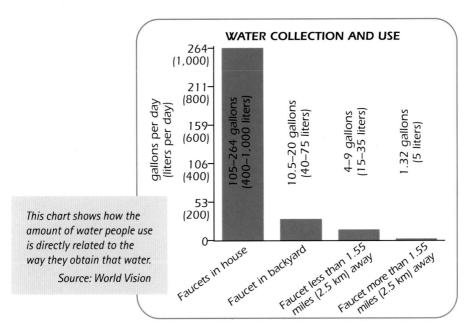

WATER COLLECTION AND USE

gallons per day (liters per day)

- 264 (1,000)
- 211 (800)
- 159 (600)
- 106 (400)
- 53 (200)
- 0

Bars:
- 105–264 gallons (400–1,000 liters) — Faucets in house
- 10.5–20 gallons (40–75 liters) — Faucet in backyard
- 4–9 gallons (15–35 liters) — Faucet less than 1.55 miles (2.5 km) away
- 1.32 gallons (5 liters) — Faucet more than 1.55 miles (2.5 km) away

This chart shows how the amount of water people use is directly related to the way they obtain that water.
Source: World Vision

WATER COSTS

Another factor that affects the amount of water people use is cost. People who have to pay more for their water tend to use it more sparingly. But, surprisingly, people often pay less for the convenience of having water piped to their homes. In 1997, people in the Philippines with household faucets paid just 11 cents for 220 gallons (1,000 liters) of water, whereas people who bought water in containers paid up to $4.74 for the same amount—making it more than 40 times more expensive!

Swaziland

The amount of water people use at home depends on how easy it is to obtain. In Swaziland, southeast Africa, people get water in different ways. In cities, a person with household faucets uses between 8–26 gallons (30–100 liters) a day. In rural areas, where water is delivered in tankers, a person uses an average of 3.4 gallons (13 liters) a day. But over two-thirds of people living in the country collect water from rivers and wells. A person carrying water home from one of these sources uses just 1.3 gallons (5 liters) a day—20 times less than a person in a nearby city.

Water and agriculture

Globally, agriculture is the world's biggest consumer of water. The water is used mainly for **irrigation** (watering) of crops, although this varies between regions. In Asia, farming accounts for 86 percent of water used, compared to 49 percent in North America and 38 percent in Europe. Irrigated land is much more productive than rain-fed farmland—although only one-sixth of the world's cropland is irrigated, it produces over one-third of the world's food.

WATER FOR MEAT

As standards of living rise in some developing countries, more people eat Western-style diets. The total world meat consumption has increased 5 times in the past 50 years. To raise livestock for meat uses a lot more water than it does to grow plant crops. You can grow 1 pound (500 grams) of wheat with about one sink full (3 gallons/13 liters) of water. Counting the water it takes to grow the grass and grain a cow eats, the water the cow drinks, and the water used for processing the meat, it takes 125 bathtubs full (2,972 gallons/11,250 liters) to produce the same weight of beef!

In less-developed countries of the world, such as Vietnam, many farmers carry irrigation water to their crops.

Irrigation issues

One of the biggest problems with irrigation is that around 60 percent of the water is wasted. That's like watering your garden with four watering cans and pouring six watering cans-worth of water down the drain! The water is lost when it leaks from faulty pipes or old canals during distribution. And when fields are watered during the day, a vast amount of water evaporates before it has a chance to soak down to the roots of the crops it was supposed to feed.

Groundwater greed

In some places, irrigation systems are draining aquifers at an alarming rate. In the United States, the huge Ogallala aquifer, which lies beneath eight U.S. states, provides an estimated third of all the country's irrigation water. This source took millions of years to fill, but farmers have been emptying it faster than rain can replenish it. Water tables are dropping by over 3.2 feet (1 meter) a year, so many farmers are looking for alternative sources of irrigation water for their crops.

This picture shows crops are being irrigated using water sprinklers. The global population of 6.5 billion is likely to increase to 8 billion by 2025. The **United Nations** predicts the amount of irrigation water needed to feed the world will double by then.

Water and industry

On average across the world, 22 percent of all water withdrawn for human use each year is used by industry, but this varies a great deal between regions. In rural regions of Africa, for example, industry uses about 8 percent of water, while in parts of Europe, industry is the biggest consumer of water at 59 percent.

WHAT DO INDUSTRIES USE WATER FOR?

Some industries that use large amounts of water produce commodities such as food, paper, chemicals, refined petroleum, and metals. For example, it takes 90 gallons (342 liters) of water to make just 2 pounds (1 kilogram) of paper. Industries use water to cool equipment that gets too hot, to wash machines, and to manufacture and process products. In the textile industry, almost all dyes and finishing chemicals are applied to fabrics in giant vats of water.

HYDROELECTRIC POWER

Half of the water used globally by industry is taken by **hydroelectric power** plants and for cooling towers in power stations. In a hydroelectric power plant, the energy in moving water is converted into electricity that supplies about one-fifth of the world's electricity needs. Hydroelectric power is a renewable, clean form of energy. It doesn't increase greenhouse gas emissions and doesn't leave dangerous radioactive materials to dispose of, as is the case with nuclear power.

*In large hydroelectric power plants, a **dam** across a river collects water in a reservoir.*

INDUSTRIAL IMPACT

When power plants and factories use water for cooling machines, it is usually returned to its source almost as clean as it was when collected. Other industrial uses of water are not so clean. In more-developed countries, there are laws preventing industrial pollution, but in many developing countries, 70 percent of factory waste is dumped straight into water supplies, polluting many rivers and aquifers. In India, groundwater in 22 major industrial areas is too contaminated to drink.

*Some of the rocks and rubble dug up by miners become **acidic** when they react with air. When water washes over these rocks, it too becomes acidic and pollutes the rivers into which it flows.*

Water Problems

Water shortages mean different things to different people. In some countries, it may mean you cannot fill your pool or water your garden for a few weeks in summer. In others, it may mean severe hardship all year round. In many countries, women and children have the job of collecting water from wells and rivers, and this has a negative impact on their health, education, and wealth (see below). When water is in short supply, people use it sparingly and hygiene practices suffer as a result.

Collecting water

The average weight of water women in Africa and Asia carry at a time is 44 pounds (20 kilograms)—the same as Europe's airport luggage allowance. Carrying heavy weights for long distances damages people's backs, especially in growing children. Collecting water also takes a lot of time, up to five hours each day. That is

In Africa, around 40 billion working hours each year are spent walking to water sources and waiting to collect water.

probably as long as you have hours of classes at school. Children miss school to collect water, or arrive late and tired, so they miss out on education that could help them find jobs later. Women cannot earn money because they have to spend time getting water.

Health and hygiene

Without adequate water supplies, people cannot maintain clean, hygienic conditions. Globally, 2.6 billion people—roughly two-fifths of the world's people—cannot wash, clean, or dispose of **sewage** properly. Because of poor sanitation and hygiene, about 40 percent of the world's 400 million school-age children are infected with intestinal worms and more than 2 million of them die from **diarrhea** each year. When people have access to clean water and soap to wash their hands, the number affected by diarrhea reduces by over 40 percent.

Elmas Kassa

Elmas Kassa is a thirteen-year-old girl living in Addis Ababa, the capital city of Ethiopia. She has never been to school because, since she was a child, she has made four trips a day to collect water for her family. Her mother has to work to buy food, so the job of collecting water is left to Elmas. Her house has no bathroom, so she bathes only once a week, and goes to the bathroom down by a river near her home. To get any privacy, she has to wait until night to go, when it is dark and people cannot see her.

Water pollution is not always visible like this. Rivers or lakes that seem clean may still be polluted by chemicals.

Pollution and disease

Pollution of water sources reduces the amount of freshwater available to us and polluted water causes disease and death. Every year, 1.7 million people die from diseases, such as diarrhea, which are carried by dirty water. Nine out of every ten people who die from dirty water are children. It is estimated that around 2 million tons (1.9 million metric tons) of waste a day pollutes our water sources, including industrial waste and chemicals, human waste, such as sewage, and agricultural waste.

Sewage

Sewage is the largest and most common pollution problem. Around 90 percent of urban sewage in the developing world flows straight into rivers, lakes, and other waterways, without being treated. Rivers downstream from large cities are often little cleaner than open sewers. The World Watch Institute estimates that 581,000 gallons (2.2 million liters) of raw sewage—enough to fill an Olympic-sized swimming pool—are dumped into the Ganges River, a main source of water in India, every two minutes.

Other sources of pollution

Individuals, agriculture, and industry use hundreds of chemicals every day. Many toxic (poisonous) chemicals are released directly into our waterways as waste, and others, such as pesticides and **fertilizers**, soak through the earth into the groundwater.

Industrial accidents also pollute water sources. In 1984, a poisonous gas leak from the U.S.-owned Union Carbide pesticide factory killed thousands of people in Bhopal, India, and left drinking water poisoned to this day. Large disasters like this make the headlines, but the build-up from smaller leaks and accidents also poses a threat to human health.

What you can do

- Dispose of used oil, paints, and other household chemicals properly. Don't empty them into drains. One drop of oil can make 7 gallons (25 liters) of water unfit for drinking!
- Apply lawn and garden chemicals sparingly, or use organic weedkillers and pesticides in your garden.

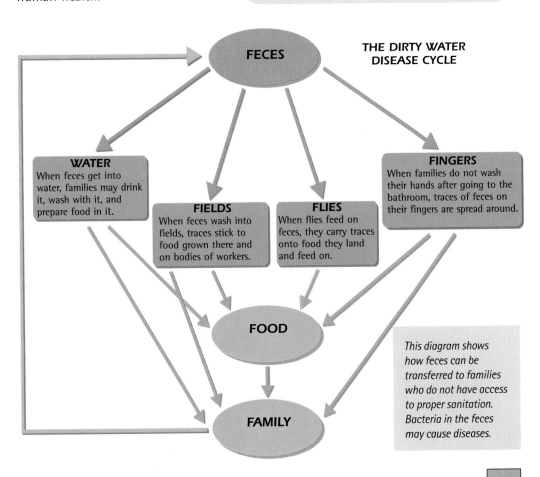

THE DIRTY WATER DISEASE CYCLE

FECES

WATER
When feces get into water, families may drink it, wash with it, and prepare food in it.

FIELDS
When feces wash into fields, traces stick to food grown there and on bodies of workers.

FLIES
When flies feed on feces, they carry traces onto food they land and feed on.

FINGERS
When families do not wash their hands after going to the bathroom, traces of feces on their fingers are spread around.

FOOD

FAMILY

This diagram shows how feces can be transferred to families who do not have access to proper sanitation. Bacteria in the feces may cause diseases.

Dams and flooding

Worldwide, there are over 45,000 dams found on nearly two-thirds of the planet's largest rivers. Together, they provide up to 40 percent of all water for irrigation, hydroelectric power, and household use. But this water often comes at a price. Some big dams **flood** people out of their towns and villages, destroy wildlife, and **habitats,** and alter river flow and water quality for people living downstream.

DISPLACEMENT

Around 80 million people have had to leave their homes to make way for large dams. Many of these families relied on river fishing for a livelihood and have to find new jobs, as well as new homes inland, and they are much worse off in the places they resettle. Dams and reservoirs reduce the flow of water downstream, which reduces fish stocks in these areas and the amount of water available for irrigation. This leads to food shortages and affects the livelihoods of thousands more fishermen.

When a new dam is being planned, communities often gather to protest, but their protests are often ignored. Here, people demonstrate against proposed dams on the Narmada River in India, 2000.

EVAPORATION

Some of the reservoirs built to supply water and large hydroelectric power plants are huge. Worldwide, their combined surface area adds up to around 120,000 miles³ (500,000 km³)—about the same size as the state of California. Vast amounts of water are lost through evaporation from this surface area, water that could have been supplying and feeding people.

The Three Gorges Dam

The Three Gorges Dam on the Yangtze River in China is the biggest hydroelectric project in the world and is scheduled for completion by 2009. As well as providing electricity, the dam will help to stop flooding of places downstream and allow large ships into the heart of China to increase trade.

However, the Three Gorges Dam will also flood over 60 miles^3 (250 km^3) of fertile farmland (about the same area as 40,000 football fields), 13 major cities, and hundreds of small villages along the river's banks. Up to 2 million people may be evacuated and left living in poorer conditions by its end.

WHAT DO YOU THINK? The Three Gorges Dam: Good or bad?

- Opponents of the Three Gorges Dam say its financial, environmental, and human costs are unacceptable.
- Supporters believe the dam is vital to prevent flooding in the area and to provide water and electricity to China's growing population.

The Three Gorges Dam should provide up to one-ninth of China's electricity and benefit many people, but it is also causing serious problems.

Salinization and subsidence

Groundwater sources take centuries to fill up and in some places, such as Bangladesh where 69 percent of drinking water is from groundwater wells, aquifers are being drained far faster than they are naturally replenishing. Draining of aquifers has serious consequences, including **salinization** and subsidence.

Large areas of land in Australia suffer from rising salt levels, leaving farms, drinking water, and rivers at risk.

SALINIZATION

Salinization is when salts accumulate in soil or water. It makes soil dry and infertile and already affects nearly one-third of the world's agricultural land. It happens in two ways. All freshwater contains a small amount of salt, but in some places, the water has a relatively high salt content. When it evaporates from fields irrigated with standing water, the salts that are left behind build up on the soil. Salinization can also happen when salt water from below the ground, or the ocean, infiltrates freshwater sources. For example, this has occurred in some coastal areas where aquifers have been drained of freshwater and salty seawater has flowed in to take its place.

CITIES AND SUBSIDENCE

Today, 48 percent of the people in the world live in cities. By 2030, this figure will rise to about 60 percent. As cities grow, the demand for water and sanitation services increases, and so urban authorities are emptying aquifers to maintain water supplies. When large amounts of groundwater have been withdrawn from certain types of rock, such as fine-grained **sediments**, the rock falls in on itself and the ground above collapses. More than 80 percent of land subsidence like this in the United States has occurred because of overpumping of groundwater.

California is sinking!

Parts of California's San Joaquin Valley have sunk by nearly 33 feet (10 meters) since the 1920s, and subsidence is a problem in many areas of California. The area gets little rainfall and for a long time, farmers and industrialists have drilled wells to get the water they need, gradually draining the region's aquifers. Subsidence causes huge cracks in the land and disruption to roads, railroads, and housing. One observer points out: "A hundred years ago, you could drill 5 feet (1.5 meters) down and water would come gushing out. Today, you have to drill 230 feet (70 meters) to find any."

Parts of 46 cities in China are sinking due to the excessive pumping of groundwater.

Water conflicts

Globally, almost half the world's population lives in river basins that cross several country borders and more than 200 rivers flow through two or more countries. The Nile River passes through ten countries, the Danube, Rhine, Niger, and Congo all flow through nine, and the Zambezi travels across eight. Increasing numbers of countries also share underground water reserves. Most countries work together to manage shared waters fairly, but many people fear that, in the future, disputes may end in conflict.

UPSTREAM AND DOWNSTREAM

Problems occur when countries around the upper stretches of a river alter the quantity or quality of water available to countries downstream. When countries upstream build dams to trap river water, divert water to irrigation projects, or overuse river water to supply cities, they reduce the flow to regions below them. When they release sewage or other waste, this contaminates water supplies and kills fish in rivers flowing through neighboring countries. Around one-fifth of the world's population is under potential threat of water supplies being altered or contaminated by upstream neighbors.

Dams and irrigation diversions on the Colorado River in the United States have affected the quantity and quality of water available downstream. Some stretches have only a trickle of water.

GEF's Nile Basin Initiative

An important step to ensuring a reliable supply of clean water is to prevent conflicts among different users. The Nile River is the longest river in the world. It runs through ten countries, six of which are among the poorest in the world and highly dependent on scarce water resources for their livelihoods.

In the past, countries upstream, such as Egypt, have built large dams, reducing water flow downstream. Since 1999, the United Nations and Global Environment Facility (GEF) have been working with countries in the region to find a way to share the water **sustainably** and fairly, and therefore prevent conflicts in the future, and also to provide funds to reduce poverty in the area.

WATER IN WARTIME

As well as being a potential cause of conflict, the destruction of water resources and facilities is also used as a weapon against enemies during times of war, or as acts of terrorism. In the Kosovo war of 1999–2000, dams, hydroelectric plants, and wells were bombed or contaminated by Serbs. In Zambia, in 1999, terrorists bombed water pipes and cut off water supplies to three million people in the city of Lusaka. Ordinary people are the first to suffer when water supplies are disrupted like this.

The conflict in Iraq that began in 2003 has left many people with a lack of running water. Here, workers in Baghdad try to repair a broken water main pipe.

29

Problem Solving

One way of conserving water is to reduce the amount we waste. Repairing underground pipes, lining canals with concrete to prevent leaks, and installing low-flush toilets that use less water are all simple ways of saving large amounts of water. Simply by mending leaky pipes, the city of São Paolo in Brazil reduced the amount of wasted water by half.

Using less water

Another way to conserve water is to use less. For example, farmers can use more efficient forms of irrigation. A simple technique is to irrigate at night when the temperatures are lower so less water is lost through evaporation. Some farms use computer-controlled drip irrigation techniques, which deliver small amounts of water directly to the roots of crop plants. New technologies also enable industries to use less water. For example, steel producers now use less than a quarter of the water they once did.

In India, heavy monsoon rains are followed by many dry months so it is vital to find innovative ways to save water. Here, rain water that has collected on the roof is being drained into a container.

Waste water recycling in Israel

Israel has limited sources of freshwater. Its surface water sources are in short supply after years of drought, and the aquifers that supply most of its drinking water are also overused. To ease the strain, Israel is building high-tech treatment plants to clean waste water from city sewage pipes so that it can be reused for irrigation. Waste water recycling now accounts for 30 percent of Israel's total supply.

Reusing and collecting water

One way of using limited water supplies more efficiently is to use lower-quality water, such as drainage water for irrigation and industrial uses. In some countries, water from washing machines or sinks is commonly reused to flush toilets. People are also finding ways of collecting and using rainwater. In some parts of India, people are beginning to catch monsoon rains on roofs and pipe them to underground stores. Frankfurt airport in Germany collects 4 million gallons (16 million liters) of rainwater on its roof for cleaning and toilet flushing.

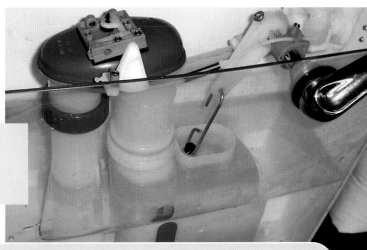

A third of all the water we use in homes goes down the toilet, so installing low-flush devices can make a real difference.

What you can do to save water

- Fix leaky faucets—a faucet leaking a drop per second loses 16 bathtubs full a month.
- Turn the faucet off while brushing your teeth.
- Save 13 gallons (50 liters) of water every time you take a shower instead of a bath.
- Adjust your toilet tank to reduce the amount of water used per flush.

Large tankers like this deliver water to water-scarce areas overland.

Making and buying water

Some countries, such as Jordan and others in the Middle East, do not have rivers or enough groundwater resources to supply people with water. They depend totally on limited rainfall and on the water that they buy in from other countries. For countries like these, **desalination**—a process that converts saltwater into freshwater—may be the main solution.

WHAT DO YOU THINK?
Exchanging water for weapons should be banned

In a "water for arms" deal in 2004, Turkey exchanged large quantities of freshwater for weapons with Israel.

- Many people believe that exchanging life-giving water for weapons of death is simply immoral.
- Others praise the deal, because it may cement a new friendship between the two countries and it provides water security for Israel.

DESALINATION DILEMMAS

Water created by desalination only adds up to about one percent of the total world water consumption, but many countries rely on it. The problems with desalination are that it uses very expensive equipment and it requires vast amounts of energy to make large amounts of clean water. It also leaves a large amount of salty brine waste that is difficult to dispose of. Because of all the greenhouse gas emissions from its energy use, desalination is also considered an environmentally-damaging process.

TRANSPORTING WATER

It is expensive to transport water into a dry country, but sometimes there are few other options. Tankers travel between water-rich countries to deliver water to places such as South Korea, Taiwan, and islands like the Bahamas, Antigua, and Mallorca. These deliveries help some communities in the short term, but they don't really make any difference to the world's water problems.

Cloud seeding

Thailand tried an innovative solution to drought problems in 2005. It sent 30 airplanes a day into the sky to carry out a process called cloud seeding—spraying chemicals into clouds to make rain fall. The chemicals encourage smaller clouds to merge, causing tiny vapor droplets to join together. The water then freezes into snow that melts into rain as it falls. Cloud seeding is a very expensive process and it is hard to prove that it works, but scientists believe that in this case, it may have increased precipitation by 5–30 percent.

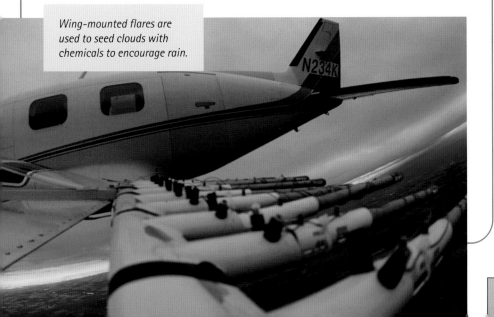

Wing-mounted flares are used to seed clouds with chemicals to encourage rain.

As India takes increasing amounts of irrigation water from the Ganges River, the huge Sunderbans wetlands area in Bangladesh is drying up, and plants and animals are losing their habitat.

Debates About Water

The way we buy and sell, use, and pollute water sources has a huge impact on people and on the environment—on plants, animals, and their habitats. For example, around 20 percent of the world's freshwater fish species (types) are **endangered** because of freshwater pollution and because water has been removed from their river or lake homes. Many people argue that humans are part of a global **ecosystem,** and when we harm wildlife or their habitats, we harm ourselves as well. Others say that we have to put human needs first.

Wetlands

Wetlands are areas of damp and boggy land, dotted with freshwater pools, usually found near coasts or riverbanks. People drain wetlands to build homes and to create farmland, or they divert wetland rivers into farms to irrigate crops. In the past 100 years, around 50 percent of the world's wetlands have been drained.

The problem is that many species of birds, amphibians, and reptiles depend on wetland habitats. When reeds and other wetland plants die, the food chains that support wildlife are damaged, and animals living there may starve. Wetlands work like giant sponges, soaking up rainwater and allowing it to drain gradually into rivers or groundwater supplies, rather than flooding land. Wetland plants also filter out sediment and dirt from polluted water, keeping the water fresh and clean for all.

Rivers and lakes

Farmers use a variety of chemicals on fields, including pesticides, which kill crop-eating insects, and fertilizers, which add nutrients to the soil. Added nutrients make food plants grow bigger and produce more fruit, vegetables, and grain. That means farmers can grow more food on their land, helping to feed increasing populations.

However, it is estimated that 50–70 percent of all nutrients in rivers and lakes has run off agricultural land. When **algae** feed on the nutrients, they reproduce and grow quickly into slimy mats that cover large areas of water. These algal blooms block light and the bacteria that feed on dead algae use up the oxygen in the water. This makes the water unfit for human consumption and, without light and oxygen, the plants, fish, and other animals in the water die.

In the last half of the 20th century, fertilizer use increased by ten times and fertilizer run-off became responsible for sights like this.

35

Privatizing water

Getting adequate water supplies to people who need it is a problem for governments across the world. It costs a lot of money to purify water and to install water pipelines and sewage systems. Some developing countries are given help by aid organizations, but this is not enough to provide water to all. Many people say the solution lies in privatization, where governments give large companies the right to control and sell water for profit.

Power to the people

In 1999, on advice from the **World Bank**, Bolivia granted a privatization lease to a group of British-led investors. This gave them control of water supplies on which more than half a million people in the poorest country in South America relied. When the company doubled and then tripled water prices, the angry people of the city of Cochabamba took action. In spring 2000, there was a general strike that left the city at a standstill for 4 days. This was followed by mass marches on the government's offices. Eventually, the people won and the government backed out of the privatization deal.

Strikers in Cochabamba wave the Bolivian flag as they protest against increased water rates.

FOR PRIVATIZATION

Supporters of privatization argue that only private companies can make the investment necessary to ensure that everyone gets access to clean water. They say that many local water authorities, run by the government or state,

Large new water treatment plants like this cost a large amount of money to build and maintain.

do not have enough money to maintain and operate water systems properly, particularly in developing countries. They argue that in many places, poor people pay up to ten times more than rich people for the same amount of water, for example, in some rural areas where tankers deliver water. They say that privatization is the only way to make water more accessible and affordable for poor people.

AGAINST PRIVATIZATION

Others argue that large companies take over the water supplies of poorer foreign countries to make quick profits, not to provide water to poor and rural communities. They say that in some developing countries, poor people face a 95 percent increase in the cost of their water after privatization, and services are cut off if people fall behind on their payments. Opponents of privatization recommend that governments run water companies and charge more to those who use most water, such as industries, to **subsidize** low-volume users, such as households and the poor.

Water rights

Human rights are equal rights and freedoms essential for human survival, freedom, and dignity that are protected by internationally agreed standards. For example, most countries in the world have signed an agreement that children have the right to an education. Should water be counted as a basic human right, or is it really a commodity to be bought and sold, like food?

In many places, there are multiple users competing for the same water supply. The issue is how to share it fairly.

RIGHT OR WRONG?

In 2002, the United Nations adopted water as a human right, saying everyone should have enough clean, physically accessible water to live and work. To define water as a right is important. It means that disputes over water must be resolved in ways that guarantee everyone can get water—not just those who can afford it, or live in the right place. It also means that governments have a duty to fulfill that right. It gives communities the right to take part in decisions about their water supply, such as where a water supply hole should be drilled and how the supply should be managed.

Others think that water, like food or oil, is a commodity, because it costs time and money, so it has to be paid for. They say that this is the only way to protect a scarce resource such as water, because people will only be more careful with water if they have to pay for it. When a commodity is in short supply, the price increases, and people use less. They say it is a simple case of supply and demand.

COMPETING INTERESTS

Sometimes, water shortages mean that difficult choices have to be made. Within a country, who has most right to water? When water is short, do farmers have more right to water than individuals? Or do industries have more right to water than farming? The debate becomes even more heated when a particular industry is owned by a foreign company. Villagers in the Palakkad district, in Kerala, India, claim that a nearby U.S.-owned Coca-Cola bottling plant is drawing more groundwater than it needs. This is reducing the amount of water available to individuals who rely on this aquifer. Coca-Cola say that their aim is to bring economic growth to the area by creating more jobs and that the reduced water supplies are due to poor rainfall, not their factory.

A protester rails against the Coca-Cola plant that villagers in Kerala, India, believe has robbed them of their groundwater supply.

39

The Future

Within 25 years, half the world's population could have trouble finding enough freshwater for drinking and irrigation. Many people fear that water problems will increase in the future because of **global warming**, which will bring more droughts to some areas and floods to others. As higher global temperatures melt glaciers, this valuable freshwater resource often ends up in the oceans.

The problem of poverty

Many people believe that the real problem is poverty, not water, and that if poor countries can establish healthy economies, they can solve water problems by buying "virtual water." For example, by importing a ton of wheat, a country is effectively importing a thousand tons of water because that is what they would have had to use to grow the wheat. Buying virtual water means a country can then give its own limited water supplies to people for drinking and sanitation, rather than agriculture.

With warmer air raising levels of evaporation in the water cycle, this will bring more rain to some areas, resulting in increased flooding in the future. This photograph shows the flooding in New Orleans caused by Hurricane Katrina, August 2005.

Small-scale hydropower plants, such as this one in Vietnam, can be located in a moving stream to bring electricity to rural or remote regions where conventional sources of power are unavailable.

Hope for the future

There are many options available to solve water issues in the future. Some solutions are simple—we need to use less water and pollute less water. Some people believe the answer lies in big ideas and technology, for example, building more desalination plants. There are even suggestions that icebergs could be towed from Antarctica to the Sahara Desert, where they would provide fresh water as they melt! Others say that small-scale plans, such as collecting water in ponds for irrigation and local hydroelectric power plants, hold the key because they are more sustainable and less damaging for the planet. The answer may lie with one or all of these solutions, but one thing is certain, water is a vital issue for us all.

Looking to the future

On World Water Day, March 22, 2005, the United Nations declared the period from 2005–2015 as an International Decade for Water, called "Water for Life." This focuses world attention on the UN's goal to help countries across the world halve the proportion of people without access to safe water by 2015. Reaching this target could cost about $20 billion a year. That sounds like a lot, but it is only about half of what Americans spend annually on pet food, or one-third of what Europeans spend on ice cream.

Statistical Information

Number of people who died from water-born diseases in 2000

Southeast Asia	699,000
Africa	608,000
Middle East*	270,000
East Asia	77,000
North and South America	55,000
Europe	15,000

*Countries such as Iran, Egypt, Ethiopia, sometimes called Eastern Mediterranean

Source: The World Health Report, WHO

Water dependency

How much water (as a percentage of total consumed) comes from outside a country's borders?

Australia	14
Bangladesh	91
Brazil	34
Central African Republic	2
Chad	65
China	1
Cuba	64
France	12
India	34
Iraq	53
Israel	55
Mexico	11
Turkey	9
UK	0
US	8

Source: FAO Aquastat, 2003

Groundwater

This table shows the amount of water withdrawn from underground resources per person in 2000.

	ft^3	m^3
Australia	5,049	143
Bangladesh	3,460	98
Brazil	2,013	57
Central African Republic	(no data)	
Chad	16	16
China	1,660	47
Cuba	14,408	408
France	3,673	104
India	7,875	223
Iraq	459	13
Israel	7,239	205
Mexico	31,854	275
Turkey	4,379	124
UK	1,483	42
US	15,256	432

Source: FAO Aquastat, 2003

Domestic water use

Amount of household water used per person in 2000

	ft³	m³
Australia	6,498	184
Bangladesh	636	18
Brazil	2,507	71
Central African Republic	177	5
Chad	212	6
China	1,130	32
Cuba	4,909	139
France	3,743	106
India	1,836	52
Iraq	2,084	59
Israel	3,673	104
Mexico	4,838	137
Turkey	2,931	83
UK	1,236	35
US	7,593	215

Source: FAO Aquastat, 2003

Sanitation

Percentage of population with access to improved sanitation in 2000

Australia	100
Bangladesh	48
Brazil	76
Central African Republic	25
Chad	29
China	40
Cuba	98
France	100
India	28
Iraq	79
Israel	(no data)
Mexico	74
Turkey	82
UK	100
US	100

Source: UNICEF

Hydroelectric power

Percentage of total hydroelectric power used by country

Australia	8
Bangladesh	6
Brazil	87
Central African Republic	(no data)
Chad	(no data)
China	16
Cuba	1
France	12
India	14
Iraq	2
Israel	0
Mexico	16
Turkey	25
UK	1
US	6

Source: World Bank Development Indicators, 2003

Bottled water

Amount of bottled water consumed by each person (average) in 2002

	Gallons	Liters
Western Europe	27	101
Eastern Europe	5	20
Asia	1.8	7
Italy	41	155
France	39	147
US	12	47
UK	7	25
Australia	4	17
Japan	3	10
New Zealand	1.3	5

Source: www.bottledwaterweb.com, www.nacsonline.com

Glossary

acidic something that has above the normal level of acid present. If soil or water is too acidic, plants cannot grow.

algae small, very simple plantlike organisms

aquifer pool of water under the ground, which can be pumped up through a well

bacteria tiny living things found in air, water, soil, and food. Some bacteria are good for us, but others can cause disease.

condenses when water turns from a gas (water vapor) to a liquid

dam barrier built across a river to stop its normal flow. Dams are used to redirect and store water in a reservoir.

dehydration loss of too much water from the body

desalination process that converts salt water into fresh water

diarrhea frequent and watery bowel movements, which can cause death due to severe dehydration (loss of water)

drought long period of time without rain or with too little rain

ecosystem community of living things, such as plants and animals, and the environment in which they live

endangered when a type of animal or plant is in danger of dying out completely

evaporate change from a liquid into a gas. For example, water evaporates to form water vapor.

fertilizer chemical powders, sprays, or liquids used to help plants grow

flood when river water overflows its banks and washes onto dry areas of land

glacier mass of ice that moves very slowly down a slope, sometimes called a river of ice

global warming rise in temperatures across the world, caused by polluting gases in the air

greenhouse gases atmospheric gases that warm the lower atmosphere by absorbing the Sun's heat

groundwater water found under the ground, in cracks, or between bits of sand, soil, and gravel

habitat natural home of a group of plants and animals. A river is one kind of habitat.

hydroelectric power electricity made using the energy of moving water

irrigation supplying water for crops, parks, golf courses, and lawns

monsoon wet season in parts of Asia and elsewhere

nutrients chemicals that plants and animals need to grow and survive

pesticides chemicals used to kill insects and other crop pests

pollution when dirt, smoke, chemicals, or other substances damage the air, soil, or water and harm living things

porous full of pores, or tiny openings. Porous rocks contain water because it soaks into these holes.

precipitation water falling to Earth in the form of rain, snow, hail, sleet, or mist

reservoir lake built by people to store water

river basin the area of land from which rainwater or streams drain into a river

run-off water that does not become absorbed by the earth but flows across the surface of the land into a stream, lake, or the ocean

salinization when salts build up in land to such a degree that they damage the soil, plants, or fresh water there

sanitation the disposal of sewage and other water waste from people's homes

sediment tiny pieces of rock and mud that often settle at the bottom of a river

sewage human waste usually carried away from people's homes in drains

subsidize grant of money, usually made by a government, to lower the price faced by producers or consumers of goods

sustainable using a resource in such a way that you don't damage it or use it up. For example, a forest where new trees are planted to replace those that are cut down for timber.

United Nations (UN) international organization formed in 1945 and comprising most of the nations of the world, to promote peace, security, and economic development

water table the level below which soil and rock are saturated with water

water vapor when water is a gas in the air. Clouds are made of condensed water vapor.

wetlands swamps and other damp areas of land

World Bank organization that lends funds to provide help to poorer member countries

Further Information

Bowden, Rob. *21st Century Debates: Water Supply* (Raintree, 2002)
This book looks at the problem of water scarcity, how we use and misuse this precious resource, and what can be done to conserve it, both now and in the future.

Clarke, Robin. *The Atlas of Water: Mapping the Global Crisis in Graphic Facts and Figures* (Earthscan Publications Ltd, 2004)
This atlas uses maps, tables, and charts to explain global water consumption, scarcity, and quality and it contains case studies about vulnerable regions such as Bangladesh.

Cosgrove, William J. and Rijsberman, Frank R. *World Water Vision: Making Water Everybody's Business* (Earthscan Publications Ltd, 2000)
This book looks at the issues in the crisis of the way the world manages its water sources and shows how water can be used effectively and productively.

Goodman, Polly. *Looking at Energy: Water Power* (Hodder Wayland, 2005)
Water Power looks at harnessing the energy of rivers and seas; how dams create electricity; tapping the warmth of the oceans; using "low technology" to provide energy in developing countries and using energy without damaging the environment.

Graham, Ian. *Earth's Precious Resources: Water* (Heinemann Library, 2003)
This book explains where water resources are found, how they are extracted, and how we use them. It answers questions such as: Why does ice float? How much water do people need to drink? Why are sea levels rising?

Parker, Steve. *Energy Files: Water* (Heinemann Library, 2003)
This book explains the formation and creation of water power from the past to its present and future uses. It examines developments in Earth's water sources and the technologies involved in the water energy industry.

Powell, Jillian. *Body Needs: Water and Fiber* (Heinemann Library, 2003)
This book looks at water and fiber as the main nutrients that the human body needs to function healthily. It explains how we get these things and what happens to the body if it gets too much or too little.

WEBSITES

You can explore the Internet to find out more about water. Websites can change, so if the links below no longer work, use a reliable search engine.

WaterAid
www.wateraid.org/usa
WaterAid is an international organization dedicated to providing safe domestic water, sanitation, and hygiene education to the world's poorest people. Their website contains a wealth of information, including case studies, news reports, campaigns, and activities.

International Rivers Network
www.irn.org
At the IRN website there is lots of information about rivers and dams, energy sources, and case studies about particular regions.

World Health Organization
www.who.int
The WHO has a section on water, sanitation, and health that looks at water resources, water related health issues, such as disease, and at solutions to water problems linked to health and hygiene.

Hydration calculator

The amount of water each person needs to drink each day varies. You can find out how much water you should be drinking using the hydration calculator at
http://www.wateraid.org/usa/get_involved/drink_more_water/

You simply enter your weight and how many minutes exercise you do each day and they will work out the number of glasses of water you should be drinking.

Index